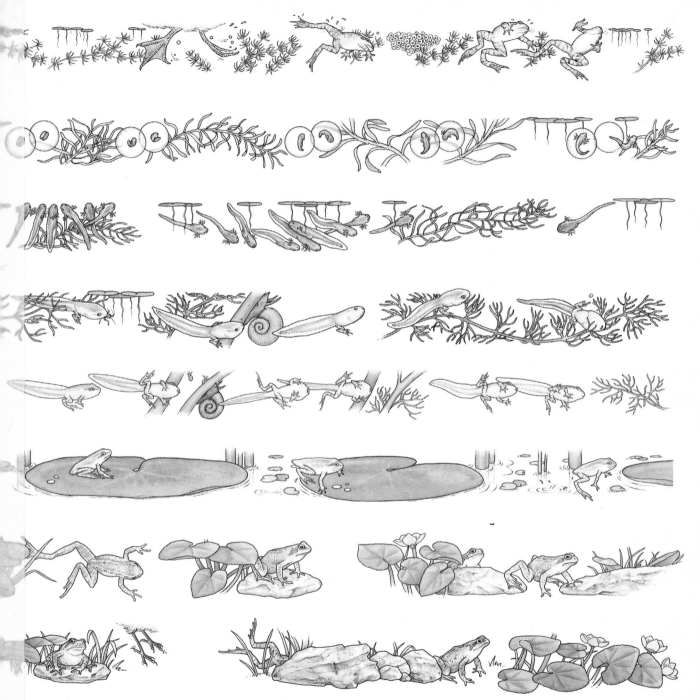

A DORLING KINDERSLEY BOOK

Written and edited by Angela Royston
Art Editor Nigel Hazle
Production Marguerite Fenn
Illustrators Sandra Pond and Will Giles

First published in Great Britain in 1991 by
Dorling Kindersley Limited, 9 Henrietta Street, London WC2E 8PS

Reprinted 1991

A CIP catalogue record for this book is available
from the British Library

ISBN 0-86318-544-4

Typesetting by Goodfellow & Egan
Colour reproduction by Scantrans, Singapore
Printed in Italy by L.E.G.O.

SEE HOW THEY GROW
FROG

photographed by
KIM TAYLOR
and JANE BURTON

DORLING KINDERSLEY
London • New York • Stuttgart

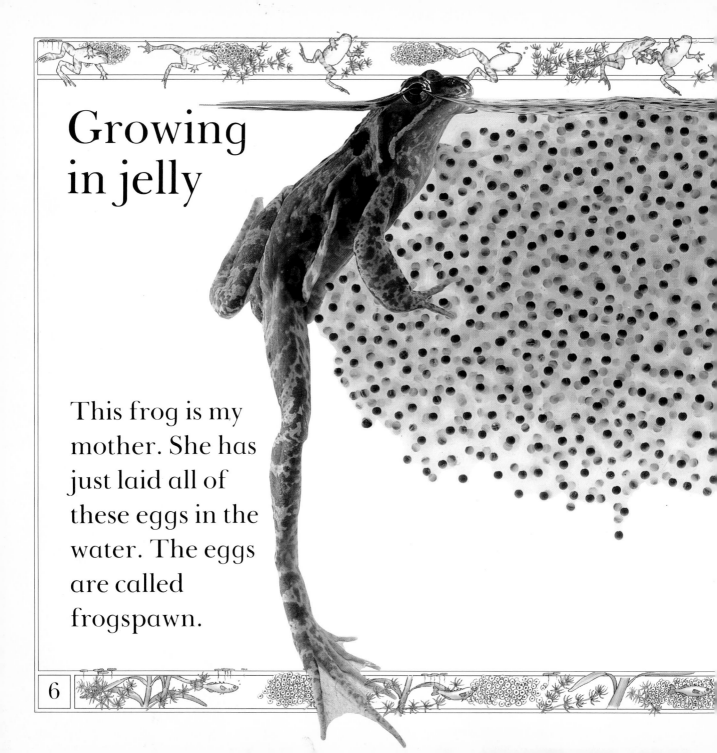

Growing
in jelly

This frog is my
mother. She has
just laid all of
these eggs in the
water. The eggs
are called
frogspawn.

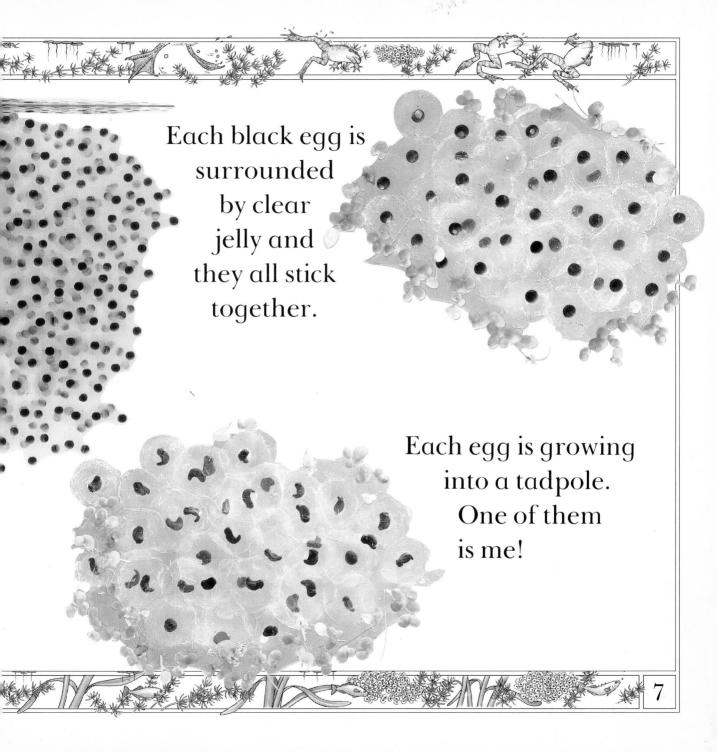

Each black egg is
surrounded
by clear
jelly and
they all stick
together.

Each egg is growing
into a tadpole.
One of them
is me!

7

Just hatched

After two weeks
I am ready to hatch.

Look at my long feathery gills. They let me breathe underwater.

I push my way through the frogspawn and swim away.

9

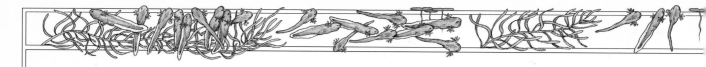

Tadpole

I am four weeks old now.
I like to swim with the
other tadpoles.

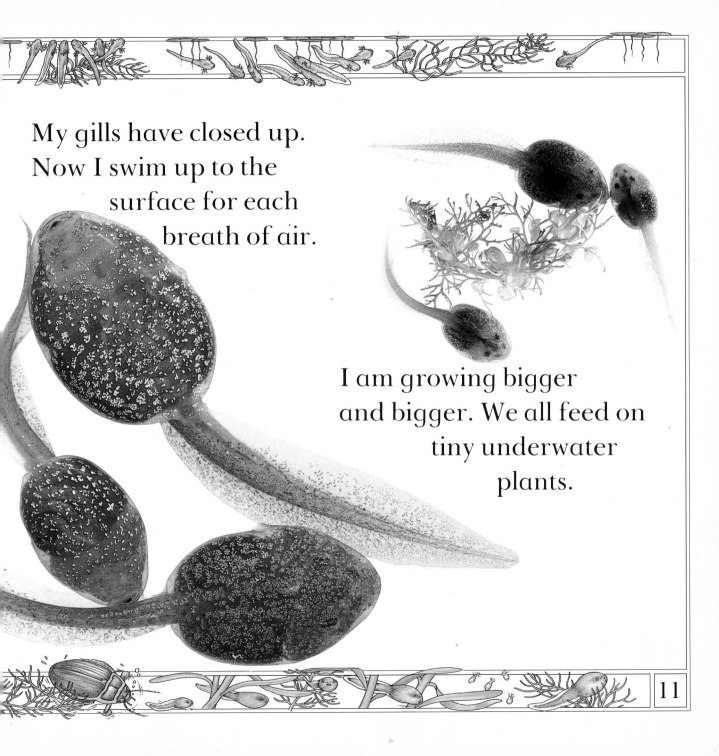

My gills have closed up.
Now I swim up to the
surface for each
breath of air.

I am growing bigger
and bigger. We all feed on
tiny underwater
plants.

Back legs first

I am six weeks old and I
have grown much bigger.
I eat plants and insects
that fall into the water.

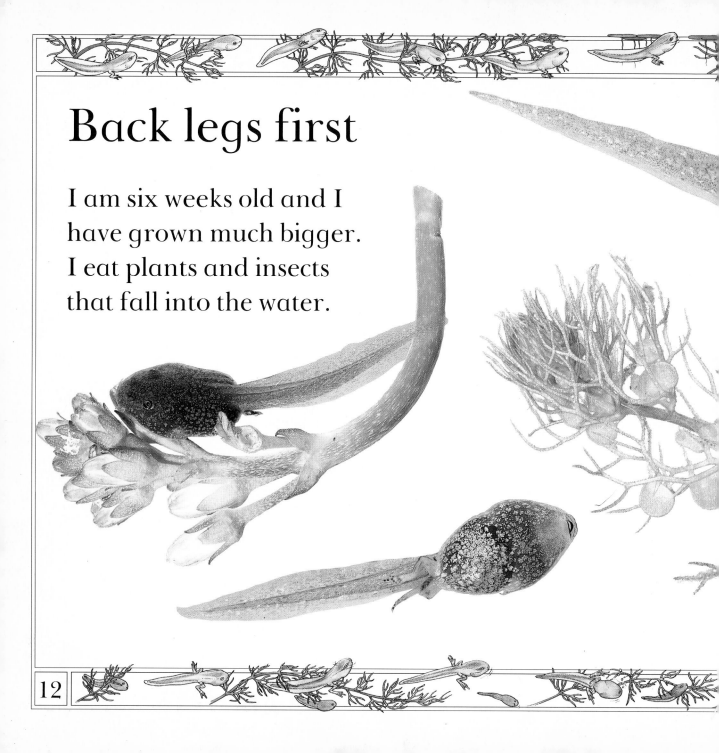

I like to swim on my own now.
My back legs are beginning to grow.
I am slowly changing into a frog.

Frogpole

I am nine
weeks old. I
am half
tadpole and
half frog.

My back legs are growing longer and now my front legs are growing too.

A frog at last

I am nearly twelve weeks
old and I am a
frog at last.

I still have a long tail which
helps me swim, but it is
getting shorter.

Here is a really big frog. Look how small I am beside her!

Out of the water

Now I am more than one year old and I spend most of my time on land.

I sit quietly watching
out for an insect to
eat. Then I shoot
out my long tongue
and snap it up.

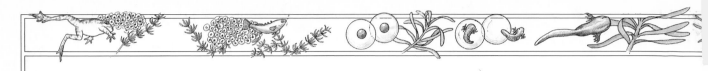

See how I grew

The egg   One day old   Four weeks old

Six weeks old   Nine weeks old

Over one year old

Twelve weeks old

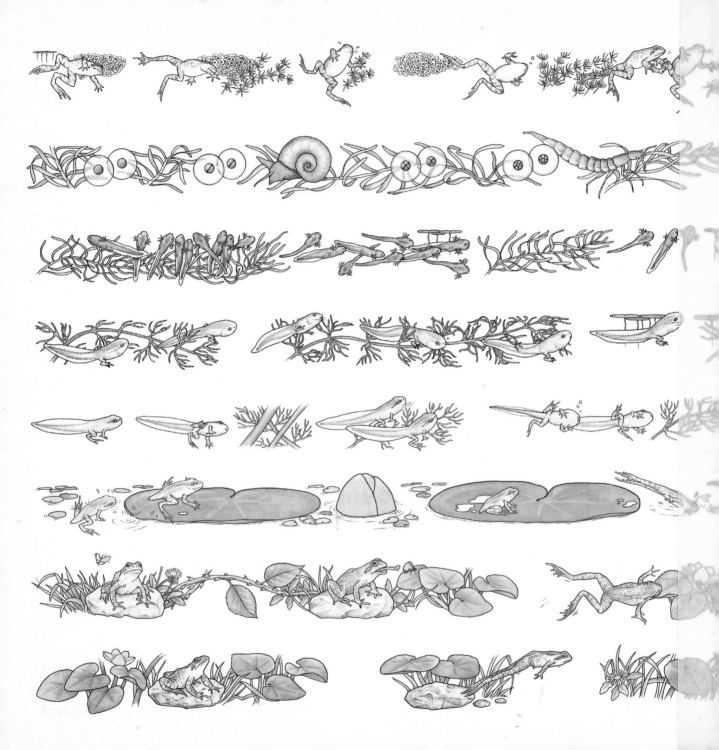